THE

CHARACTER OF JESUS

FORBIDDING HIS
POSSIBLE CLASSIFICATION WITH MEN.

BY

HORACE BUSHNELL.

NEW YORK:
THE CHAUTAUQUA PRESS,
C. L. S. C. DEPARTMENT,
805 BROADWAY.
1888.

PUBLISHER'S ADVERTISEMENT.

————•••————

IN this little volume we reprint, with consent of the Author, the tenth chapter of his Treatise, NATURE AND THE SUPERNATURAL.

This chapter, taken as a sketch of the self-evidencing, superhuman character of Christ, has attracted much attention ; and we have been solicited, many times over, in the various notices and reviews of the book, as well as by private readers, to give it to the public by itself. This, too, we do the more readily, that it makes a complete whole by itself, and is in a style to be read by multitudes who probably will not undertake to master the more elaborate and difficult argument, of which it is only a subordinate member.

CONTENTS.

CONTENTS.

THE
CHARACTER OF JESUS.

IT is the grand peculiarity of the sacred writings, that they deal in supernatural events and transactions, and show the fact of a celestial institution finally erected on earth, which is fitly called the kingdom of God; because it shows Him reigning, as a Regenerator and Restorer of the broken order of the world. Christianity is, in this view, no mere scheme of doctrine, or of ethical practice, but is instead a kind of miracle, a power out of nature and above, descending into it; a historically supernatural movement on the world, that is visibly entered into it, and organized to be an institution in the person of Jesus Christ. He, therefore, is the central figure and power, and with him the entire fabric either stands or falls.

To this central figure, then, we now turn ourselves; and, as no proof beside the light is necessary to show that the sun shines, so we shall find that Jesus proves himself by his own self-evidence. The simple inspection of his life and character will suffice to show that he cannot be classified with mankind (man though he be), any more than what we call his miracles can be classified with mere nat-

ural events. The simple demonstrations of his life
and spirit are the sufficient attestation of his own
profession, when he says—" I am from above "—" I
came down from heaven."

Let us not be misunderstood. We do not assume
the truth of the narrative by which the manner and
facts of the life of Jesus are reported
to us ; for this, by the supposition, is
the matter in question. We only as-
sume the representations themselves, as being just
what they are, and discover their necessary truth,
in the transcendent, wondrously self-evident, picture of divine excellence and beauty exhibited in
them. We take up the account of Christ, in the
New Testament, just as we would any other ancient
writing, or as if it were a manuscript just brought
to light in some ancient library. We open the
book, and discover in it four biographies of a certain remarkable character, called Jesus Christ. He
is miraculously born of Mary, a virgin of Galilee,
and declares himself, without scruple, that he came
out from God. Finding the supposed history made
up, in great part, of his mighty acts, and not being
disposed to believe in miracles and marvels, we
should soon dismiss the book as a tissue of absurdities too extravagant for belief, were we not struck
with the sense of something very peculiar in the
character of this remarkable person. Having our
attention arrested thus by the impression made on

We assume
nothing report-
ed of him to be
true.

our respect, we are put on inquiry, and the more we study it, the more wonderful, as a character, it appears. And before we have done, it becomes, in fact, the chief wonder of the story; lifting all the other wonders into order and intelligent proportion round it, and making one compact and glorious wonder of the whole picture; a picture shining in its own clear sunlight upon us, as the truest of all truths—Jesus, the Divine Word, coming out from God, to be incarnate with us, and be the vehicle of God and salvation to the race.

On the single question, therefore, of the more than human character of Jesus, we propose, in perfect confidence, to rest a principal argument for Christianity as a supernatural institution; for, if there be in Jesus a character which is not human, then has something broken into the world that is not of it, and the spell of unbelief is broken.

Not that Christianity might not be a supernatural institution, if Jesus were only a man; for many prophets and holy men, as we believe, have brought forth to the world communications that are not from themselves, but were received by inspirations from God. There are several grades, too, of the supernatural, as already intimated; the supernatural human, the supernatural prophetic, the supernatural demonic and angelic, the supernatural divine. Christ, we shall see, is the supernatural manifested in the highest grade or order; viz., the divine.

We observe, then, as a first peculiarity at the root
of his character, that he begins life with a perfect
youth. His childhood is an unspotted,
and, withal, a kind of celestial flower.
The notion of a superhuman or celestial
childhood, the most difficult of all
things to be conceived, is yet successfully drawn
by a few simple touches. He is announced before-
hand as "that Holy Thing"; a beautiful and
powerful stroke, to raise our expectation to the
level of a nature so mysterious. In his childhood,
everybody loves him. Using words of external
description, he is shown growing up in favor with
God and man, a child so lovely and beautiful, that
heaven and earth appear to smile upon him together. So, when it is added that the child grew
and waxed strong in spirit, filled with wisdom, and,
more than all, that the grace or beautifying power
of God was upon him, we look, as on the unfolding
of a sacred flower, and seem to scent a fragrance
wafted on us from other worlds. Then, at the age
of twelve, he is found among the great learned men
of the day, the doctors of the temple, hearing what
they say, and asking them questions. And this,
without any word that indicates forwardness or
pertness in the child's manner, such as some Christian Rabbi, or silly and credulous devotee, would
certainly have added. The doctors are not offended, as by a child too forward or wanting in modesty;

The only character that has a perfect youth.

they are only amazed that such a degree of understanding can dwell in one so young and simple.
His mother finds him there among them, and begins to expostulate with him. His reply is very
strange ; it must, she is sure, have some deep meaning that corresponds with his mysterious birth, and
the sense he has ever given her of a something
strangely peculiar in his ways ; and she goes home
keeping his saying in her heart, and guessing vainly
what his thought may be. Mysterious, holy secret !
which this mother hides in her bosom ; that her
holy thing, her child whom she has watched, during
the twelve years of his celestial childhood, now begins to speak of being " about his Father's busi-
ness," in words of dark enigma, which she can not
fathom.

Now we do not say, observe, that there is one
word of truth in these touches of narrative. We
only say that, whether they be fact or
fiction, here is given the sketch of a The picture
stands by it-
perfect and sacred childhood, not of a self.
simple, lovely, ingenuous, and properly human
childhood, such as the poets love to sketch, but of
a sacred and celestial childhood. In this respect,
the early character of Jesus is a picture that stands
by itself. In no other case, that we remember, has
it ever entered the mind of a biographer, in drawing
a character, to represent it as beginning with a spotless childhood. The childhood of the great human

characters, if given at all, is commonly represented, according to the uniform truth, as being more or less contrary to the manner of their mature age ; and never as being strictly one with it, except in those cases of inferior eminence where the kind of distinction attained to is that of some mere prodigy, and not a character of greatness in action, or of moral excellence. In all the higher ranges of character, the excellence portrayed is never the simple unfolding of a harmonious and perfect beauty contained in the germ of childhood, but it is a character formed by a process of rectification, in which many follies are mended and distempers removed ; in which confidence is checked by defeat, passion moderated by reason, smartness sobered by experience. Commonly a certain pleasure is taken in showing how the many wayward sallies of the boy are, at length, reduced by discipline to the character of wisdom, justice, and public heroism, so much admired.

Besides, if any writer, of almost any age, will undertake to describe, not merely a spotless, but a superhuman or celestial childhood, not having the reality before him, he must be somewhat more than human himself, if he does not pile together a mass of clumsy exaggerations, and draw and overdraw, till neither heaven nor earth can find any verisimilitude in the picture.

Neither let us omit to notice what ideas the Rabbis and learned doctors of this age were able, in fact, to furnish, when setting forth a remarkable childhood. Thus Josephus, drawing on the teachings of the Rabbis, *The absurd pictures given of infant prodigies.* tells how the infant Moses, when the king of Egypt took him out of his daughter's arms, and playfully put the diadem on his head, threw it pettishly down and stamped on it. And when Moses was three years old, he tells us that the child had grown so tall, and exhibited such a wonderful beauty of countenance, that people were obliged, as it were, to stop and look at him as he was carried along the road, and were held fast by the wonder, gazing till he was out of sight. See, too, what work is made of the childhood of Jesus himself, in the Apocryphal gospels. These are written by men of so nearly the same era, that we may discover, in their embellishments, what kind of a childhood it was in the mere invention of the time to make out. While the gospels explicitly say that Jesus wrought no miracles till his public ministry began, and that he made his beginning in the miracle of Cana, these are ambitious to make him a great prodigy in his childhood. They tell how, on one occasion, he pursued in his anger, the other children, who refused to play with him, and turned them into kids ; how, on another, when a child accidentally ran against him, he was angry, and killed him by his mere word ; how, on another, Jesus had a dispute with his teacher over the alphabet, and when the teacher struck him, how he crushed him, withered his arm, and threw him down dead. Finally, Joseph tells Mary that they must keep him within doors, for everybody perishes against whom he is excited. His mother sends him to the well for water, and having broken his pitcher, he brings the water in his cloak. He goes into a dyer's shop, when the dyer is out, and throws all the cloths he finds into a vat of one color ; but, when they are taken out, behold, they are all dyed of the precise color that was ordered. He commands a palm-tree to stoop down and let him pluck the fruit, and it obeys. When he is carried down into Egypt, all the idols fall down wherever he passes, and the lions and leopards gather round him in a harmless company. This the Gospel of the Infancy gives, as a picture of the wonderful childhood of Jesus. How unlike that holy flower of paradise, in the true gospels, which a few simple touches make to bloom in beautiful self-evidence before us!

————

Passing now to the character of Jesus in his maturity, we discover, at once, that there is an element *Jesus the only* in it which distinguishes it from all *great character* human characters, viz., innocence. By *that holds a foot-* *ing of innocence.* this we mean, not that he is actually sinless ; that will be denied, and, therefore, must not here be assumed. We mean that, viewed ex-

ternally, he is a perfectly harmless being, actuated
by no destructive passions, gentle to inferiors, doing
ill or injury to none. The figure of a Lamb, which
never was, or could be applied to any of the great
human characters, without an implication of weakness fatal to all respect, is yet, with no such effect,
applied to him. We associate weakness with innocence, and the association is so powerful, that no
human writer would undertake to sketch a great
character on the basis of innocence, or would even
think it possible. We predicate innocence of infancy ; but to be a perfectly harmless, guileless
man, never doing ill even for a moment, we consider
to be the same as to be a man destitute of spirit and
manly force. But Christ accomplished the impossible. Appearing in all the grandeur and majesty of
a superhuman manhood, he is able still to unite the
impression of innocence, with no apparent diminu-
tion of his sublimity. It is, in fact, the distinctive
glory of his character, that it seems to be the natural unfolding of a divine innocence ; a pure celestial childhood, amplified by growth. We feel the
power of this strange combination, but we have so
great difficulty in conceiving it, or holding our
minds to the conception, that we sometimes subside
or descend to the human level, and empty the character of Jesus of the strange element unawares.
We read, for example, his terrible denunciations
against the Pharisees, and are shocked by the vio-

lent, fierce sound they have on our mortal lips ; not perceiving that the offence is in us, and not in him. We should suffer no such revulsion, did we only conceive them bursting out, as words of indignant grief, from the surcharged bosom of innocence ; for there is nothing so bitter as the offence that innocence feels, when stung by hypocrisy and a sense of cruelty to the poor. So, when he drives the money-changers from the temple, we are likely to leave out the only element that saves him from a look of violence and passion. Whereas, it is the very point of the story, not that he, as by mere force, can drive so many men, but that so many are seen retiring before the moral power of one, a mysterious being, in whose face and form the indignant flush of innocence reveals a tremendous feeling, they can no wise comprehend, much less are able to resist.

Accustomed to no such demonstrations of vigor and decision in the innocent human characters, and having it as our way to set them down contemptuously, without further consideration, as

" Incapable and shallow innocents,"—

we turn the indignant fire of Jesus into a fire of malignity ; whereas, it should rather be conceived that Jesus here reveals his divinity, by what so powerfully distinguishes God himself, when he clothes his goodness in the tempests and thunders of nature. Decisive, great, and strong, Christ is yet all this, even the more sublimely, that he is invested, withal, in the lovely, but humanly feeble garb of innocence. And that this is the true conception, is clear, in the fact that no one ever thinks of him as weak, and no one fails to be somehow impressed with a sense of innocence by his life. When his enemies are called to show what evil or harm he hath done, they can specify nothing, save that he has offended their bigotry. Even Pilate, when he gives him up, confesses that he finds nothing in him to blame, and, shuddering with apprehensions he cannot subdue, washes his hands to be clear of the innocent blood! Thus he dies, a being holy, harmless, undefiled. And when he hangs, a bruised flower, drooping on his cross, and the sun above is dark, and the earth beneath shudders with pain, what have we in this funeral grief of the worlds, but a fit honor paid to the sad majesty of his divine innocence?

————

We pass now to his religious character, which, we shall discover, has the remarkable distinction that it proceeds from a point exactly opposite to that which is the root or radical element in the religious character of men. Human piety begins with repentance. It is the effort of a being, implicated in wrong and writhing under the stings of guilt, to come unto God. The most

The only religious character that disowns repentance.

righteous, or even self-righteous men, blend expressions of sorrow and vows of new obedience with their exercises. But Christ, in the character given him, never acknowledges sin. It is the grand peculiarity of his piety that he never regrets anything that he has done or been ; expresses, nowhere, a single feeling of compunction, or the least sense of unworthiness. On the contrary, he boldly challenges his accusers, in the question—Which of you convinceth me of sin ? and even declares, at the close of his life, in a solemn appeal to God, that he has given to men, unsullied, the glory divine that was deposited in him.

Now the question is not whether Christ was, in fact, the faultless being, assumed in his religious character. All we have to notice here is, that he makes the assumption, makes it not only in words, but in the very tenor of his exercises themselves, and that by this fact his piety is radically distinguished from all human piety. And no mere human creature, it is certain, could hold such a religious attitude, without shortly displaying faults that would cover him with derision, or excesses and delinquencies that would even disgust his friends. Piety without one dash of repentance, one ingenuous confession of wrong, one tear, one look of contrition, one request to heaven for pardon—let any one of mankind try this kind of piety, and see how long it will be ere his righteousness will prove itself to be the most impudent conceit! how long before his passions sobered by no contrition, his pride kept down by no repentance, will tempt him into absurdities that will turn his pretenses to mockery! No sooner does any one of us begin to be self-righteous, than he begins to fall into outward sins that shame his conceit. But, in the case of Jesus, no such disaster follows. Beginning with an impenitent or unrepentant piety, he holds it to the end, and brings no visible stain upon it.

Now, one of two things must be true. He was either sinless, or he was not. If sinless, what greater, more palpable exception to the law of human development, than that a perfect and stainless being has for once lived in the flesh! If not, which is the supposition required of those who deny every thing above the range of human development, then we have a man taking up a religion without repentance, a religion not human, but celestial, a style of piety never taught him in his childhood, and never conceived or attempted among men : more than this, a style of piety, withal, wholly unsuited to his real character as a sinner, holding it as a figment of insufferable presumption to the end of life, and that in a way of such unfaltering grace and beauty, as to command the universal homage of the human race! Could there be a wider deviation from all we know of mere human development?

He was also able perfectly to unite elements of character, that others find the greatest difficulty in uniting, however unevenly and partial-ly. He is never said to have laughed, and yet he never produces the impression of austerity, moroseness, sadness, or even of being unhappy. On the contrary, he is described as one that appears to be commonly filled with a sacred joy ; "rejoicing in spirit," and leaving to his disciples, in the hour of his departure, the bequest of his joy—"that they might have my joy fulfilled in themselves." We could not long endure a human being whose face was never moved by laughter, or relaxed by humorous play. What sympathy could we have with one who appears, in this manner, to have no human heart? We could not even trust him. And yet we have sympathy with Christ ; for there is somewhere in him an ocean of deep joy, and we see that he is, in fact, only burdened with his sympathy for us to such a degree, that his mighty life is overcast and oppressed by the charge he has undertaken. His lot is the lot of privation ; he has no powerful friends ; he has not even where to lay his head. No human being could appear in such a guise, without occupying us much with the sense of his affliction. We should be descending to him, as it were, in pity. But we never pity Christ, never think of him as struggling with the disadvantages of a lower level, to surmount them. In

He unites characters difficult to be united.

fact, he does not allow us, after all, to think much of his privations. We think of him more as a being of mighty resources, proving himself only the more sublimely, that he is in the guise of destitution. He is the most unworldly of beings, having no desire at all for what the earth can give, too great to be caught with any longing for its benefits, impassible even to its charms, and yet there is no ascetic sourness or repugnance, no misanthropic distaste in his manner ; as if he were bracing himself against the world to keep it off. The more closely he is drawn to other worlds, the more fresh and susceptible is he to the humanities of this. The little child is an image of gladness, which his heart leaps forth to embrace. The wedding and the feast and the funeral have all their cord of sympathy in his bosom. At the wedding he is clothed in congratulation, at the feast in doctrine, at the funeral in tears ; but no miser was ever drawn to his money, with a stronger desire, than he to worlds above the world.

Men undertake to be spiritual, and they become ascetic ; or, endeavoring to hold a liberal view of the comforts and pleasures of society, they are soon buried in the world, and slaves to its fashions ; or, holding a scrupulous watch to keep out every particular sin, they become legal, and fall out of liberty ; or, charmed with the noble and heavenly liberty, they run to negligence and irresponsible living ; so the earnest become violent, the fervent fanatical

and censorious, the gentle waver, the firm turn big-
ots, the liberal grow lax, the benevolent ostentatious.
Poor human infirmity can hold nothing steady.
Where the pivot of righteousness is broken, the
scales must needs slide off their balance. Indeed,
it is one of the most difficult things which a cultiva-
ted Christian can attempt, only to sketch a theoretic
view of character, in its true justness and proportion,
so that a little more study, or a little more self-ex-
perience, will not require him to modify it. And
yet the character of Christ is never modified, even
by a shade of rectification. It is one and the same
throughout. He makes no improvements, prunes no
extravagances, returns from no eccentricities. The
balance of his character is never disturbed, or read-
justed, and the astounding assumption on which it is
based is never shaken, even by a suspicion that he
falters in it.

There is yet another point related to this, in
which the attitude of Jesus is even more distinct
from any that was ever taken by man,
and is yet triumphantly sustained. I
speak of the astonishing pretensions
asserted concerning his person. Similar pretensions have sometimes been assumed by maniacs, or
insane persons, but never, so far as I know, by persons in the proper exercise of their reason. Certain
it is that no mere man could take the same attitude
of supremacy towards the race, and inherent affinity

The astonish-
ing pretensions
of Jesus.

or oneness with God, without fatally shocking the confidence of the world by his effrontery. Imagine a human creature saying to the world—" I came forth from the Father "—" ye are from beneath, I am from above "; facing all the intelligence and even the philosophy of the world, and saying, in bold assurance—" behold, a greater than Solomon is here "—" I am the light of the world "—" the way, the truth, and the life "; publishing to all peoples and religions —" No man cometh to the Father, but by me "; promising openly in his death—" I will draw all men unto me "; addressing the Infinite Majesty, and testifying—" I have glorified thee on the earth "; calling to the human race—" Come unto me "; " follow me "; laying his hand upon all the dearest and most intimate affections of life, and demanding a precedent love—" he that loveth father or mother more than me, is not worthy of me." Was there ever displayed an example of effrontery and spiritual conceit so preposterous? Was there ever a man that dared put himself on the world in such pretensions?—as if all light was in him; as if to follow him and be worthy of him was to be the conclusive or chief excellence of mankind! What but mockery and disgust does he challenge as the certain reward of his audacity! But no one is offended with Jesus on this account, and what is a sure test of his success, it is remarkable that, of all the readers of the gospel, it probably never even occurs to one in a hundred thousand, to blame his conceit, or the egregious vanity of his pretensions.

Nor is there any thing disputable in these pretensions, least of all, any trace of myth or fabulous traditions. They enter into the very web of his ministry, so that if they are extracted and nothing left transcending mere humanity, nothing at all is left. Indeed, there is a tacit assumption, continually maintained, that far exceeds the range of these formal pretensions. He says—"I and the Father that sent me." What figure would a man present in such language—I and the Father? He goes even beyond this, and apparently without any thought of excess or presumption ; classing himself with the Infinite Majesty in a common plural, he says— *We* will come unto him, and make *our* abode with him. Imagine any, the greatest and holiest of mankind, any prophet, or apostle, saying *we*, of himself and the Great Jehovah ! What a conception did he give us concerning himself, when he assumed the necessity of such information as this—" my Father is greater than I "; and above all, when he calls himself, as he often does, in a tone of condescension—" the Son of Man." See him also on the top of Olivet, looking down on the guilty city and weeping words of compassion like these—imagine some man weeping over London or New York, in the like—" How often would I have gathered thy children together as a hen doth gather

His pretensions enter also into his actions.

her chickens under her wings, and ye would not!" See him also in the supper, instituting a rite of remembrance for himself, a scorned, outcast man, and saying—"this is my body"—"this do in remembrance of me."

I have dwelt thus on the transcendent pretensions of Jesus, because there is an argument here for his superhumanity, which can not be resisted. For eighteen hundred years, these prodigious assumptions have been published and preached to a world that is quick to lay hold of conceit, and bring down the lofty airs of pretenders, and yet, during all this time, whole nations of people, composing as well the learned and powerful as the ignorant and humble, have paid their homage to the name of Jesus, detecting never any disagreement between his merits and his pretensions, offended never by any thought of his extravagance. In which we have absolute proof that he practically maintains his amazing assumptions! Indeed it will even be found that, in the common apprehension of the race, he maintains the merit of a most peculiar modesty, producing no conviction more distinctly, than that of his intense lowliness and humility. His worth is seen to be so great, his authority so high, his spirit so celestial, that instead of being offended by his pretensions, we take the impression of one in whom it is even a condescension to breathe our air. I say not that his friends

Nobody offended by these pretensions.

and followers take this impression, it is received as naturally and irresistibly by unbelievers. I do not recollect any skeptic or infidel who has even thought to accuse him as a conceited person, or to assault him in this, the weakest and absurdest, if not the strongest and holiest, point of his character.

Come now, all ye that tell us in your wisdom of the mere natural humanity of Jesus, and help us to find how it is, that he is only a natural development of the human ; select your best and wisest character ; take the range, if you will, of all the great philosophers and saints, and choose out one that is most competent ; or if, perchance, some one of you may imagine that he is himself about upon a level with Jesus (as we hear that some of you do), let him come forward in this trial and say—" follow me "—" be worthy of me "—" I am the light of the world "—" ye are from beneath, I am from above "—" behold a greater than Solomon is here "; take on all these transcendent assumptions, and see how soon your glory will be sifted out of you by the detective gaze, and darkened by the contempt of mankind ! Why not ? is not the challenge fair ? Do you not tell us that you can say as divine things as he ? Is it not in you, too, of course, to do what is human ? are you not in the front rank of human developments ? do you not rejoice in the power to rectify many mistakes and errors in the words of Jesus ? Give us

What mere man could support such pretensions?

then this one experiment, and see if it does not prove to you a truth that is of some consequence ; viz., that you are a man, and that Jesus Christ is— more.

————

But there is also a passive side to the character of Jesus which is equally peculiar, and which likewise demands our attention. I recollect no really great character in history, excepting such as may have been formed under Christianity, that can properly be said to have united the passive virtues, or to have considered them any essential part of a finished character. Socrates comes the nearest to such an impression, and therefore most resembles Christ in the submissiveness of his death. It does not appear, however, that his mind had taken this turn previously to his trial, and the submission he makes to the public sentence is, in fact, a refusal only to escape from the prison surreptitiously ; which he does, partly because he thinks it the duty of every good citizen not to break the laws, and partly, if we judge from his manner, because he is detained by a subtle pride ; as if it were something unworthy of a grave philosopher, to be stealing away, as a fugitive, from the laws and tribunals of his country. The Stoics, indeed, have it for one of their great principles, that the true wisdom of life consists in a passive power, viz., in being able to bear suffering rightly. But they

Peculiar in the passive virtues.

mean by this, the bearing of suffering so as not to feel it ; a steeling of the mind against sensibility, and a raising of the will into such power as to drive back the pangs of life, or shake them off.   But this, in fact, contains no allowance of passive virtue at all ; on the contrary, it is an attempt so to exalt the active powers, as even to exclude every sort of passion, or passivity.   And Stoicism corresponds, in this respect, with the general sentiment of the world's great characters.   They are such as like to see things in the heroic vein, to see spirit and courage breasting themselves against wrong, and, where the evil can not be escaped by resistance, dying in a manner of defiance.   Indeed it has been the impression of the world generally, that patience, gentleness, readiness to suffer wrong without resistance, is but another name for weakness.

But Christ, in opposition to all such impressions, manages to connect these non-resisting and gentle passivities with a character of the severest grandeur and majesty ; and, what is more, convinces us that no truly great character can exist without them.

Observe him, first, in what may be called the common trials of existence.   For if you will put a character to the severest of all tests, see whether it can bear without faltering, the little common ills and hindrances of life.   Many a man will go to his martyrdom, with a spirit of firmness and heroic

Does not falter in the common trials of existence.

composure, whom a little weariness or nervous exhaustion, some silly prejudice, or capricious opposition, would, for the moment, throw into a fit of vexation, or ill-nature. Great occasions rally great principles, and brace the mind to a lofty bearing, a bearing that is even above itself. But trials that make no occasion at all, leave it to show the goodness and beauty it has in its own disposition. And here precisely is the superhuman glory of Christ as a character, that he is just as perfect, exhibits just as great a spirit, in little trials as in great ones. In all the history of his life, we are not able to detect the faintest indication that he slips or falters. And this is the more remarkable, that he is prosecuting so great a work, with so great enthusiasm; counting it his meat and drink, and pouring into it all the energies of his life. For when men have great works on hand, their very enthusiasm runs to impatience. When thwarted or unreasonably hindered, their soul strikes fire against the obstacles they meet, they worry themselves at every hindrance, every disappointment, and break out in stormy and fanatical violence. But Jesus, for some reason, is just as even, just as serene, in all his petty vexations, and hindrances, as if he had nothing on hand to do. A kind of sacred patience invests him everywhere. Having no element of crude will mixed with his work, he is able, in all trial and opposition, to hold a condition of serenity above the clouds, and let them sail under him, without ever obscuring the sun. He is poor, and hungry, and weary, and despised, insulted by his enemies, deserted by his friends, but never disheartened, never fretted or ruffled.

You see, meantime, that he is no Stoic ; he visibly feels every such ill as his delicate and sensitive nature must, but he has some sacred and sovereign good present, to mingle with his pains, which, as it were, naturally and without any self-watching, allays them. He does not seem to rule his temper, but rather to have none ; for temper, in the sense of passion, is a fury that follows the will, as the lightnings follow the disturbing forces of the winds among the clouds ; and accordingly, where there is no self-will to roll up the clouds and hurl them through the sky, the lightnings hold their equilibrium, and are as though they were not.

As regards what is called pre-eminently his passion, the scene of martyrdom that closes his life, it is easy to distinguish a character in it His passion no mere human martyr-dom. which separates it from all mere human martyrdoms. Thus, it will be observed, that his agony, the scene in which his suffering is bitterest and most evident, is, on human principles, wholly misplaced. It comes before the time, when as yet there is no arrest, and no human prospect that there will be any. He is at large, to go where he pleases, and in perfect outward safety.

His disciples have just been gathered round him in a scene of more than family tenderness and affection. Indeed it is but a very few hours since that he was coming into the city, at the head of a vast procession, followed by loud acclamations, and attended by such honors as may fitly celebrate the inaugural of a king. Yet here, with no bad sign apparent, we see him plunged into a scene of deepest distress, and racked, in his feeling, with a more than mortal agony. Coming out of this, assured and comforted, he is shortly arrested, brought to trial and crucified; where, if there be any thing questionable in his manner, it is in the fact that he is even more composed than some would have him to be, not even stooping to defend himself or vindicate his innocence. And when he dies, it is not as when the martyrs die. They die for what they have said, and remaining silent will not recant. He dies for what he has not said, and still is silent.

By the misplacing of his agony thus, and the strange silence he observes when the real hour of agony is come, we are put entirely at fault on natural principles. But it was not for him to wait, as being only a man, till he is arrested, and the hand of death *His agony misplaced, taken as being only a man's.* is upon him, then to be nerved by the occasion to a show of victory. He that was before Abraham, must also be before his occasions. In a time of safety, in a cool hour of retirement, unaccountably to his friends, he falls into a dreadful contest and struggle of mind ; coming out of it finally to go through his most horrible tragedy of crucifixion, with the serenity of a spectator!

Why now this so great intensity of sorrow? why this agony? Was there not something unmanly in it, something unworthy of a really great soul? Take him to be only a man, and there probably was ; nay, if he were a woman, the same might be said. But this one thing is clear, that no one of mankind, whether man or woman, ever had the sensibility to suffer so intensely ; even showing the body, for the mere struggle and pain of the mind, exuding and dripping with blood. Evidently there is something mysterious here ; which mystery is vehicle to our feeling, and rightfully may be, of something divine. What, we begin to ask, should be the power of a superhuman sensibility? and how far should the human vehicle shake under such a power? How too should an innocent and pure spirit be exercised, when about to suffer, in his own person, the greatest wrong ever committed?

It is, humanly speaking, excessive.

Besides there is a vicarious spirit in love ; all love inserts itself vicariously into the sufferings and woes and, in a certain sense, the sins of others, taking them on itself as a burden. How then, if perchance Jesus should be divine, an embodiment of God's love in the

The pathology is divine.

world — how should he feel, and by what signs of feeling manifest his sensibility, when a fallen race are just about to do the damning sin that crowns their guilty history; to crucify the only perfect being that ever came into the world; to crucify even him, the messenger and representative to them of the love of God, the deliverer who has taken their case and cause upon him! Whosoever duly ponders these questions, will find that he is led away, more and more, from any supposition of the mere mortality of Jesus. What he looks upon, he will more and more distinctly see to be the pathology of a superhuman anguish. It stands, he will perceive, in no mortal key. It will be to him the anguish, visibly, not of any pusillanimous feeling, but of holy character itself; nay, of a mysteriously transcendent, or somehow divine character.

But why did he not defend his cause and justify his innocence in the trial? Partly because he had the wisdom to see that there really was *His defence before Pilate all that could be made.* and could be no trial, and that one who undertakes to plead with a mob, only mocks his own virtue, throwing words into the air that is already filled with the clamors of prejudice. To plead innocence in such a case, is only to make a protestation, such as indicates fear, and is really unworthy of a great and composed spirit. A man would have done it, but Jesus did not. Besides, there was a plea of innocence in the manner of Jesus, and the few very significant words that he dropped, that had an effect on the mind of Pilate, more searching and powerful than any formal protestations. And the more we study the conduct of Jesus during the whole scene, the more shall we be satisfied that he said enough ; the more admire the mysterious composure, the wisdom, the self-possession, and the superhuman patience of the sufferer. It was visibly the death-scene of a transcendent love. He dies not as a man, but rather as some one might, who is mysteriously more and higher. So thought aloud the hard-faced soldier—"Truly this was the Son of God." As if he had said—"I have seen men die—this is not a man. They call him Son of God—he can not be less." Can he be less to us ?

But Christ shows himself to be a superhuman character, not in the personal traits only, exhibited in his life, but even more sublimely in the undertakings, works, and teachings, by which he proved his Messiahship.

He undertakes what is humanly impossible.

Consider then the reach of his undertaking ; which, if he was only a man, shows him to have been the most extravagant and even wildest of all human enthusiasts. Contrary to every religious prejudice of his nation and even of his time, contrary to the comparatively narrow and exclusive religion of Moses itself, and to all his training under it, he undertakes to organize a kingdom of God, or kingdom of heaven on earth. His purpose includes a new moral creation of the race—not of the Jews only and of men proselyted to their covenant, but of the whole human race. He declared thus, at an early date in his ministry, that many shall come from the east and the west and sit down with Abraham, and Isaac and Jacob, in the kingdom of God ; that the field is the world ; and that God so loves the world, as to give for it his only-begotten Son. He also declared that his gospel shall be published to all nations, and gave his apostles their commission to go into all the world, and publish his gospel to every creature.

Here, then, we have the grand idea of his mission —it is to new-create the human race and restore it to God, in the unity of a spiritual king- He assumes to dom. And upon this single fact, Rein- dom of God hard erects a complete argument for among men. his extra human character ; going into a formal review of all the great founders of states and most celebrated lawgivers, the great heroes and defenders of nations, all the wise kings and statesmen, all the philosophers, all the prophet founders of religions, and discovering as a fact that no such thought as this, or nearly proximate to this, had ever before been taken up by any living character in history ; showing also how it had happened to every other great character, however liberalized by culture, to be limited in some way to the interest of his own people, or empire, and set in opposition, or antagonism, more or less decidedly, to the rest of the world. But to Jesus alone, the simple Galilean carpenter, it happens otherwise ; that, never having seen a map of the world in his whole life, or heard the name of half the great nations on it, he undertakes, coming out of his shop, a scheme as much vaster and more difficult than that of Alexander, as it proposes more and what is more divinely benevolent! This thought of a universal kingdom, cemented in God—why, the immense Roman empire of his day, constructed by so many ages of war and conquest, is a bauble in comparison, both as regards the extent and the cost! And yet the rustic tradesman of Galilee propounds even this for his errand, and that in a way of assurance, as simple and quiet, as if the immense reach of his plan were, in fact, a matter to him of no consideration.

Nor is this all ; there is included in his plan, what, to any mere man, would be yet more remote His plan covers ages of time. from the possible confidence of his frailty ; it is a plan as universal in time, as it is in the scope of its objects. It does not expect to be realized in a lifetime, or even in many centuries to come. He calls it understandingly, his grain of mustard-seed ; which, however, is to grow, he declares, and overshadow the whole earth. But the courage of Jesus, counting a thousand years to be only a single day, is equal to the run of his work. He sees a rock of stability, where men see only frailty and weakness. Peter himself, the impulsive and always unreliable Peter, turns into rock and becomes a great foundation, as he looks upon him. "On this rock," he says, "I will build my church, and the gates of hell shall not prevail against it." His expectation, too, reaches boldly out beyond his own death ; that, in fact, is to be the seed of his great empire—"except a corn of wheat fall into the ground and die, it abideth," he says, "alone." And if we will see with what confidence and courage he adheres to his plan, when the time of his death approaches—how far he is from giving it up as lost, or as an exploded vision of his youthful enthusiasm—we have only to observe his last interview with the two sisters of Bethany, in whose hospitality he was so often comforted. When the box of precious ointment is broken upon his head, which Judas reproves as a useless expense, he discovers a sad propriety or even prophecy, in what the woman has done, as connected with his death, now at hand. But it does not touch his courage, we perceive, or the confidence of his plan, or even cast a shade on his prospect. "Let her alone. She hath done what she could. She is come aforehand to anoint my body to the burying. Verily I say unto you, wheresoever this gospel shall be preached

throughout the whole world, this also that this
woman hath done shall be told for a memorial of
her." Such was the sublime confidence he had in
a plan that was to run through all future ages, and
would scarcely begin to show its fruit during his
own lifetime.

Is this great idea then, which no man ever before
conceived, the raising of the whole human race to God,

Such attempts
not human.

a plan sustained with such evenness of
courage, and a confidence of the world's
future so far transcending any human example—is
this a human development? Regard the benevolence of it, the universality of it, the religious
grandeur of it, as a work readjusting the relations
of God and his government with men—the cost, the
length of time it will cover, and the far-off date of
its completion—is it in this scale that a Nazarene
carpenter, a poor uneducated villager, lays out his
plans and graduates the confidence of his undertakings? There have been great enthusiasts in the
world, and they have shown their infirmity by lu-
natic airs, appropriate to their extravagance. But
it is not human, we may safely affirm, to lay out
projects transcending all human ability, like this of
Jesus, and which cannot be completed in many
thousands of years, doing it in all the airs of sobri-
ety, entering on the performance without parade,
and yielding life to it firmly as the inaugural of its
triumph. No human creature sits quietly down to

a perpetual project, one that proposes to be executed only at the end, or final harvest of the world. That is not human, but divine.

Passing now to what is more interior in his ministry, taken as a revelation of his character, we are struck with another distinction, viz., He takes rank that he takes rank with the poor, and with the humblest orders of grounds all the immense expectations society. of his cause, on a beginning made with the lowly and dejected classes of the world. He was born to the lot of the poor. His manners, tastes, and intellectual attainments, however, visibly outgrew his condition, and that in such a degree that, if he had been a mere human character, he must have suffered some painful distaste for the kind of society in which he lived. The great, as we perceive, flocked to hear him, and sometimes came even by night to receive his instructions. He saw the highest circles of society and influence open to him, if he only desired to enter them. And, if he was a properly human character, what virtuous, but rising young man would have had a thought of impropriety, in accepting the elevation within his reach ; considering it as the proper reward of his industry and the merit of his character—not to speak of the contempt for his humble origin, and his humble associates, which every upstart person, of only ordinary virtue, is so commonly seen to manifest. Still he adheres to the poor, and makes them the object of his ministry. And what is more peculiar, he visibly has a kind of interest in their society, which is wanting in that of the higher classes ; perceiving, apparently, that they have a certain aptitude for receiving right impressions, which the others have not. They are not the wise and prudent, filled with the conceit of learning and station, but they are the ingenuous babes of poverty, open to conviction, prepared, by their humble lot, to receive thoughts and doctrines in advance of their age. Therefore he loves the poor, and, without descending to their low manners, he delights to be identified with them. He is more assiduous in their service than other men have been in serving the great. He goes about on foot, teaching them and healing their sick ; occupying his great and elevated mind, for whole years, with details of labor and care, which the nurse of no hospital had ever laid upon him—insanities, blind eyes, fevers, fluxes, leprosies, and sores. His patients are all below his level and unable to repay him, even by a breath of congenial sympathy ; and nothing supports him but the consciousness of good which attends his labors.

Meantime, consider what contempt for the poor had hitherto prevailed among all the great statesmen and philosophers of the world. The poor were not society, or any part of society. They were only the con-

No great social architect ever saw the wisdom of it.

veniences and drudges of society; appendages of luxury and state, tools of ambition, material to be used in the wars. No man who had taken up the idea of some great change or reform in society, no philosopher who had conceived the notion of building up an ideal state or republic, ever thought of beginning with the poor. Influence was seen to reside in the higher classes, and the only hope of reaching the world, by any scheme of social regeneration, was to begin with them, and through them operate its results. But Christ, if we call him a philosopher, and, if he is only a man, we can call him by no higher name, was the poor man's philosopher; the first and only one that had ever appeared. Seeing the higher circles open to him, and tempted to imagine that, if he could once get footing for his doctrine among the influential and the great, he should thus secure his triumph more easily, he had yet no such thought. He laid his foundations, as it were, below all influence, and, as men would judge, threw himself away.

And precisely here did he display a wisdom and character totally in advance of his age. Eighteen centuries have passed away, and we now seem just beginning to understand the transcendent depth of this feature in his mission and his character. We appear to be just waking up to it as a discovery, that the blessing and upraising of the masses are the fundamental interest of society—a discovery, however, which is only a proof that the life of Jesus has at length begun to penetrate society and public history. It is precisely this which is working so many and great changes in our times, giving liberty and right to the enslaved many, seeking their education, encouraging their efforts by new and better hopes, producing an aversion to war, which has been the fatal source of their misery and depression, and opening, as we hope, a new era of comfort, light, and virtue in the world. It is as if some higher and better thought had visited our race—which higher thought is in the life of Jesus. The schools of all the philosophers are gone, hundreds of years ago, and all their visions have died away into thin air ; but the poor man's philosopher still lives, bringing up his poor to liberty, light, and character, and drawing the nations on to a brighter and better day.

At the same time, the more than human character of Jesus is displayed also in the fact that, identifying himself thus with the poor, he is yet able to do it, without eliciting any feelings of partisanship in them. To one who will be at the pains to reflect a little, nothing will seem more difficult than this; to become the patron of a class, a downtrodden and despised class, without rallying in them a feeling of intense malignity. And that for the reason, partly, that no patron, how-

And still he raises no partisan feeling.

ever just or magnanimous, is ever quite able to suppress the feelings of a partisan in himself. A little ambition, pricked on by a little abuse, a faint desire of popularity playing over the face of his benevolence, and tempting him to loosen a little of illnature, as tinder to the passions of his sect—something of this kind is sure to kindle some fire of malignity in his clients.

Besides, men love to be partisans. Even Paul and Apollos and Peter had their sects or schools, glorying in one against another. With all their efforts, they could not suppress ^{No human leader in this.} a weakness so contemptible. But no such feeling could ever get footing under Christ. If his disciples had forbidden one to heal in the name of Jesus, because he followed not with them, he gently rebuked them, and made them feel that he had larger views than to suffer any such folly. As the friend of the poor and oppressed class, he set himself openly against their enemies, and chastised them as oppressors, with the most terrible rebukes. He exposed the absurdity of their doctrine, and silenced them in argument ; he launched his thunderbolts against their base hypocrisies ; but it does not appear that the populace ever testified their pleasure, even by a cheer, or gave vent to any angry emotion under cover of his leadership. For there was something still, in the manner and air of Jesus, which made them feel it to be inappropriate, and even made it impossible. It was as if some being were here, taking their part, whom it were even an irreverence to applaud, much more to second by any partisan clamor. They would as soon have thought of cheering the angel in the sun, or of rallying under him as the head of their faction.

On one occasion, when he had fed the multitudes by a miracle, he saw that their national superstitions were excited, and that, regarding him as the Messiah predicted in the Scriptures, they were about to take him by force and make him their king ; but this was a national feeling, not the feeling of a class. Its root was superstition, not hatred. His triumphal entry into Jerusalem, attended by the acclamations of the multitude, if this be not one of the fables or myths, which our modern criticism rejects, is yet no demonstration of popular faction, or party animosity. Robbing it of its mystical and miraculous character, as the inaugural of the Messiah, it has no real signification. In a few hours, after all, these hosannas are hushed, Jesus is alone and forsaken, and the very multitudes he might seem to have enlisted, are crying " Crucify him! " On the whole, it cannot be said that Jesus was ever popular. He was followed at times, by great multitudes of people, whose love of the marvellous worked on their superstitions, to draw them after him. They came also to be cured of their diseases. They knew him as their friend. But there was yet something in him that forbade their low and malignant feelings gathering into a conflagration round him. He presents, indeed, an instance that stands alone in history, as God at the summit of the worlds, where a person has identified himself with a class, without creating a faction, and without becoming a popular character.

———

Consider him next as a teacher ; his method and manner, and the other characteristics of his excellence, apart from his doctrine. That will be distinctly considered in another place.

First of all, we notice the perfect originality and independence of his teaching. We have a great many men who are original, in the sense of being originators within a certain boundary of educated thought. But the originality of Christ is uneducated. That he draws nothing from the stores of learning, can be seen at a glance. The impression we have in reading his instructions, justifies to the letter, the language of his contemporaries, when they say, "this man hath never learned." There is nothing in any of his allusions, or forms of speech that indicates learning. Indeed, there is nothing in him that belongs to his age or country—no one opinion, or taste, or prejudice. The attempts that have been made, in a way of establishing his mere natural manhood, to show that he borrowed his sentiments

Original and independent as no man is.

from the Persians and the eastern forms of religion, or that he had been intimate with the Essenes, and borrowed from them, or that he must have been acquainted with the schools and religions of Egypt, deriving his doctrine from them—all attempts of the kind have so palpably failed, as not even to require a deliberate answer.

If he is simply a man, as we hear, then he is most certainly a new and singular kind of man, never before heard of ; one who visibly is quite as great a miracle in the world as if he were not a man. We can see for ourselves, in the simple directness and freedom of his teachings, that whatever he advances is from himself. Shakspeare, for instance, whom we name as being probably the most creative and original spirit the world has ever produced, one of the class, too, that are called self-made men, is yet tinged, in all his works, with human learning. His glory is, indeed, that so much of what is great in history and historic character, lives and appears in his dramatic creations. He is the high-priest, we sometimes hear, of human nature. But Christ, understanding human nature so as to address it more skilfully than he, derives no help from historic examples. He is the high-priest, rather, of the divine nature, speaking as one that has come out from God, and has nothing to borrow from the world. It is not to be detected, by any sign, that the human sphere in which he moved imparted any thing to him. His teachings are just as full of divine nature, as Shakspeare's of human.

Neither does he teach by the human methods. He does not speculate about God, as a school professor, drawing out conclusions by a practice Teaches by no on words, and deeming that the way of human method. proof; he does not build up a frame of evidence from below, by some constructive process, such as the philosophers delight in; but he simply speaks of God and spiritual things as one who has come out from Him, to tell us what he knows. And his simple telling brings us the reality; proves it to us in its own sublime self-evidence; awakens even the consciousness of it in our own bosom; so that formal arguments or dialectic proofs offend us by their coldness, and seem, in fact, to be only opaque substances set between us and the light. Indeed, he makes even the world luminous by his words—fills it with an immediate and new sense of God, which nothing has ever been able to expel. The incense of the upper world is brought out, in his garments, and flows abroad, as perfume, on the poisoned air.

At the same time, he never reveals the infirmity so commonly shown by human teachers, when they veer a little from their point, or turn their doctrine off by shades of variation, Warped by no desire to gain to catch the assent of multitudes. He assent. never conforms to an expectation, even of his friends. When they look to find a great prophet in him, he offers nothing in the modes of the prophets. When they ask for places of distinction in his kingdom, he rebukes their folly, and tells them he has nothing to give, but a share in his reproaches and his poverty. When they look to see him take the sword as the Great Messiah of their nation, calling the people to his standard, he tells them he is no warrior and no king, but only a messenger of love to lost men ; one that has come to minister and die, but not to set up or restore the kingdom. Every expectation that rises up to greet him, is repulsed ; and yet, so great is the power of his manner, that multitudes are held fast, and can not yield their confidence. Enveloped as he is in the darkest mystery, they trust him still ; going after him, hanging on his words, as if detained by some charmed influence, which they can not shake off or resist. Never was there a teacher that so uniformly baffled every expectation of his followers, never one that was followed so persistently.

Again, the singular balance of character displayed in the teachings of Jesus, indicates an exemption Comprehensive, under no human conditions. from the standing infirmity of human nature. Human opinions are formed under a law that seems to be universal. First, two opposite extremes are thrown up, in two opposite leaders or parties ; then a third party enters, trying to find what truth they both are endeavoring to vindicate, and settle thus a view of the subject, that includes the truth and clears the one-sided extremes, which opposing words or figures, not yet measured in their force, had produced. It results, in this manner, that no man, even the broadest in his apprehensions, is ever at the point of equilibrium as regards all subjects. Even the ripest of us are continually falling into some extreme, and losing our balance, afterward to be corrected by some other who discovers our error, or that of our school.

But Christ was of no school or party, and never went to any extreme—words could never turn him to a one-sided view of any thing. This is the remarkable fact that distinguishes him from any other known teacher of the world. Having nothing to work out in a word-process, but every thing clear in the simple intuition of his superhuman intelligence, he never pushes himself to any human eccentricity. It does not even appear that he is trying, as we do, to balance opposites and clear extravagances, but he does it, as one who can not imagine a one-sided view of any thing. He is never a radical, never a conservative. He will not allow his disciples to deny him before kings and governments, he will not let them renounce their allegiance to Cæsar. He exposes the oppressions of the Pharisees in Moses' seat, but, encouraging no factious resistance, says—" do as they command you." His position as a reformer was universal ; according to his principles almost nothing, whether in church or state, or in social life, was right, and

Could not hold a one-sided view

yet he is thrown into no antagonism against the world. How a man will do, when he engages only in some one reform, acting from his own human force ; the fuming, storming phrenzy, the holy rage and tragic smoke of his violence, how he kindles against opposition, grows bitter and restive because of delay, and finally comes to maturity in a character thoroughly detestable—all this we know. But Christ, with all the world upon his hands, and a reform to be carried in almost every thing, is yet as quiet and cordial, and as little in the attitude of bitterness or impatience, as if all hearts were with him, or the work already done ; so perfect is the balance of his feeling, so intuitively moderated is it by a wisdom not human.

We can not stay to sketch a full outline of this particular and sublime excellence, as it was displayed in his life. It will be seen as clearly in a single comparison or contrast, as in many, or in a more extended inquiry. Take, then, for an example, what may be observed in his open repugnance to all superstition, combined with his equal repugnance to what is commonly praised as a mode of liberality. He lived in a superstitious age and among a superstitious people. He was a person of low education, and nothing, as we know, clings to the uneducated mind with the tenacity of a superstition. Lord Bacon, for example, a man certainly of the very highest in-

Clear of all the current superstitions.

tellectual training, was yet harmed by superstitions too childish to be named with respect, and which clung to him despite of all his philosophy, even to his death. But Christ, with no learned culture at all, comes forth out of Galilee, as perfectly clean of all the superstitions of his time, as if he had been a disciple, from his childhood, of Hume or Strauss. " You children of superstition think," he says, " that those Galileans, whose blood Pilate mingled with their sacrifices, and those eighteen upon whom the tower in Siloam fell, must have been monsters, to suffer such things. I tell you, nay ; but except ye repent, ye shall all likewise perish." To another company he says—" You imagine, in your Pharisaic and legal morality, that the Sabbath of Moses stands in the letter ; but I tell you that the Sabbath is made for man, and not man for the Sabbath ; little honor, therefore, do you pay to God, when you teach that it is not lawful to do good on this day. Your washings are a great point, you tithe herbs and seeds with a sanctimonious fidelity, would it not be as well for you. teachers of the law, to have some respect to the weightier matters of justice, faith, and benevolence ? " Thus, while Socrates, one of the greatest and purest of human souls, a man who has attained to many worthy conceptions of God, hidden from his idolatrous countrymen, is constrained to sacrifice a cock' to Esculapius, the uneducated Jesus lives and dies superior to every superstition of his time ; believing nothing because it is believed, respecting nothing because it is sanctified by custom and by human observance. Even in the closing scene of his life, we see his learned and priestly associates refusing to go into the judgment-hall of Caiaphas, lest they should be ceremonially defiled and disqualified for the feast ; though detained by no scruple at all as regards the instigation of a murder! While he, on the other hand, pitying their delusions, prays for them from his cross—" Father, forgive them, for they know not what they do."

And yet Christ is no liberal, never takes the ground or boasts the distinction of a liberal among

But no liberalist.

his countrymen, because it is not a part of his infirmity, in discovering an error here, to fly to an excess there. His ground is charity, not liberality ; and the two are as wide apart in their practical implications, as adhering to all truth, and being loose in all. Charity holds fast the minutest atoms of truth, as being precious and divine, offended by even so much as a thought of laxity. Liberality loosens the terms of truth ; permitting easily and with careless magnanimity variations from it ; consenting, as it were, in its own sovereignty, to overlook or allow them ; and subsiding thus, ere long, into a licentious indifference to all truth, and a general defect of responsibility in regard to it. Charity extends allowance to men ;

liberality, to falsities themselves. Charity takes the truth to be sacred and immovable ; liberality allows it to be marred and maimed at pleasure. How different the manner of Jesus in this respect from that unreverent, feeble laxity, that lets the errors be as good as the truths, and takes it for a sign of intellectual eminence, that one can be floated comfortably in the abysses of liberalism. "Judge not," he says, in holy charity, "that ye be not judged"; and again, in holy exactness, "whosoever shall break, or teach to break, one of these least commandments shall be least in the kingdom of God"—in the same way, "he that is not with us is against us"; and again, "he that is not against us is for us"—in the same way also, "ye tithe mint, anise, and cummin"; and again, "these things ought ye to have done, and not to leave the other undone"—once more, too, in the same way, "he that is without sin, let him cast the first stone"; and again, "go, and sin no more." So magnificent and sublime, so plainly divine, is the balance of Jesus. Nothing throws him off the centre on which truth rests ; no prejudice, no opposition, no attempt to right a mistake, or rectify a delusion, or reform a practice. If this be human, I do not know, for one, what it is to be human.

Again, it is a remarkable and even superhuman distinction of Jesus, that, while he is advancing doctrines so far transcending His simplicity is perfect. all deductions of philosophy, and opening mysteries

that defy all human powers of explication, he is yet
able to set his teachings in a form of simplicity, that
accommodates all classes of minds. And this, for
the reason that he speaks directly to men's convictions themselves, without and apart from any learned
and curious elaboration, such as the uncultivated
can not follow. No one of the great writers of an-
tiquity had even propounded, as yet, a doctrine of
virtue which the multitude could understand. It
was taught as being το καλον [the fair], or το
πρεπον [the becoming], or something of that nature, as distant from all their apprehensions, and as
destitute of motive power, as if it were a doctrine
of mineralogy. Considered as a gift to the world
at large, it was the gift of a stone, not of bread.
But Jesus tells them directly, in a manner level to
their understanding, what they want, what they
must do and be, to inherit eternal life, and their
inmost convictions answer to his words. Besides,
his doctrine is not so much a doctrine as a biogra-
phy, a personal power, a truth all motivity, a love
walking the earth in the proximity of a mortal fel-
lowship. He only speaks what goes forth as a feeling and a power in his life, breathing into all hearts.
To be capable of his doctrine, only requires that
the hearer be a human creature, wanting to know
the truth.

Call him, then, who will, a man, a human teacher ;
what human teacher ever came down thus upon the

soul of the race, as a beam of light from the skies—
pure light, shining directly into the
visual orb of the mind, a light for all that ^{Shining as pure light.}
live, a full transparent day, in which
truth bathes the spirit as an element. Others talk
and speculate about truth, and those who can may
follow ; but Jesus is the truth, and lives it, and if
he is a mere human teacher, he is the first who was
ever able to find a form for truth, at all adequate to
the world's uses. And yet the truths he teaches
outreach all the doctrines of all the philosophers of
the world. He excels them a hundred-fold more,
in the scope and grandeur of his doctrine, than he
does in his simplicity itself.

Is this human, or is it plainly divine? If you
will see what is human, or what the wisdom of humanity would ordain, it is this—exactly
what the subtle and accomplished Celsus, ^{Adequately teaches God}
the great adversary of Christianity in its ^{even to the humble.}
original promulgation, alleges for one of
his principal arguments against it. "Woollen
manufacturers," he says, "shoemakers and curriers,
the most uneducated and boorish of men are zeal-
ous advocates of this religion ; men who can not
open their mouths before the learned, and who only
try to gain over the women and children in fami-
lies." * And again, what is only the same objection,
under a different form, assuming that religion, like

* Neander's Memorials of Christian Life, p. 19.

a philosophy, must be for the learned, he says, "He must be void of understanding who can believe that Greeks and barbarians, in Asia, Europe, and Lybia—all nations to the ends of the earth—can unite in one and the same religious doctrine." * So also, Plato says, "it is not easy to find the Father and Creator of all existence, and when he is found it is impossible to make him known to all." † "But exactly this," says Justin Martyr, "is what our Christ has effected by his power." And Tertullian, also, glorying in the simplicity of the gospel, as already proved to be a truly divine excellence, says, "Every Christian artisan has found God, and points him out to thee, and in fact, shows thee every thing which is sought for in God, although Plato maintains that the Creator of the world is not easily found, and that, when he is found, he can not be made known to all." ‡ Here, then, we have Christ against Celsus, and Christ against Plato. These agree in assuming that we have a God, whom only the great can mount high enough in argument to know. Christ reveals a God whom the humblest artisan can teach, and all mankind embrace, with a faith that unifies them all.

Again, the morality of Jesus has a practical superiority to that of all human teachers, in the

* Neander's Memorials of Christian Life, p. 33.

† Timæus.

‡ Neander's Memorials of Christian Life, p. 19.

fact that it is not an artistic, or theoretically elaborated scheme, but one that is propounded in precepts that carry their own evidence, and are, in fact, great spiritual laws ordained by God, in the throne of religion. He did not draw long arguments to settle what the *summum bonum* is, and then produce a scheme of ethics to correspond. He did not go into the vexed question, what is the foundation of virtue? and hang a system upon his answer. Nothing falls into an artistic shape, as when Plato or Socrates asked what kind of action is beautiful in action? reducing the principles of morality to a form as difficult for the uncultivated, as the art of sculpture itself. Yet Christ excels them all in the beauty of his precepts, without once appearing to consider their beauty. He simply comes forth telling us, from God, what to do, without deducing any thing in a critical way; and yet, while nothing has ever yet been settled by the critics and theorizing philosophers, that could stand fast and compel the assent of the race, even for a year, the morality of Christ is about as firmly seated in the convictions of men, as the law of gravity in their bodies.

This morality is not artistic.

He comes into the world full of all moral beauty, as God of physical; and as God was not obliged to set himself to a course of æsthetic study, when he created the forms and landscapes of the world, so Christ comes to his rules, by no critical practice

in words.   He opens his lips, and the creative glory
of his mind pours itself forth in living

But intuitive and original.

precepts—Do to others as ye would that
others should do to you—Blessed are
the peacemakers—Smitten upon one cheek, turn the
other—Resist not evil—Forgive your enemies—Do
good to them that hate you—Lend not, hoping to
receive—Receive the truth as little children. Omitting all the deep spiritual doctrines he taught, and
taking all the human teachers on their own ground,
the ground of preceptive morality, they are seen at
once to be meager and cold ; little artistic inventions, gleams of high conceptions caught by study,
having about the same relation to the Christian
morality that a statue has to the flexibility, the self-
active force, and flushing warmth of man, as he
goes forth in the image of his Creator, to be the
reflection of His beauty and the living instrument
of his will.   Indeed, it is the very distinction of
Jesus that he teaches, not a verbal, but an original,
vital, and divine morality.   He does not dress up a
moral picture and ask you to observe its beauty, he
only tells you how to live ; and the most beautiful
characters the world has ever seen, have been those
who received and lived his precepts without once
conceiving their beauty.

Once more, it is a high distinction of

Never anxious for success.

Christ's character, as seen in his teachings, that he is never anxious for the success of his doctrine. Fully conscious of the fact that the world is against him, scoffed at, despised, hated, alone too, in his cause, and without partisans that have any public influence, no man has ever been able to detect in him the least anxiety for the final success of his doctrine. He is never jealous of contradiction. When his friends display their dulness and incapacity, or even when they forsake him, he is never ruffled or disturbed. He rests on his words, with a composure as majestic as if he were sitting on the circle of the heavens. Now the consciousness of truth, we are not about to deny, has an effect of this nature in every truly great mind. But when it has had an effect so complete? What human teacher, what great philosopher, has not shown some traces of anxiety for his school, that indicated his weakness; some pride in his friends, some dislike of his enemies, some traces of wounded ambition, when disputed or denied? But here is a lone man, a humble, uneducated man, never schooled into the elegant fiction of an assumed composure, or practised in the conventional digni- ties of manners, and yet, finding all the world against him, the world does not rest on its axle more firmly than he upon his doctrine. Questioned by Pilate what he means by truth, it is enough to answer—" He that is of the truth heareth my voice." If this be human, no other man of the race, we are sure, has ever dignified humanity by a like example.

Such is Christ as a teacher. When has the world seen a phenomenon like this; a lonely uninstructed youth, coming forth amid the moral darkness of Galilee, even more distinct from his age, and from every thing around him, than a Plato would be rising up alone in some wild tribe in Oregon, assuming thus a position at the head of the world, and maintaining it, for eighteen centuries, by the pure self-evidence of his life and doctrine! Does he this by the force of mere human talent or genius? If so, it is time that we begin to look to genius for miracles; for there is really no greater miracle.

There is yet one other and more inclusive distinction of the character of Jesus, which must not
be omitted, and which sets him off more
Raised and made sacred by familiarity. widely from all the mere men of the race, just because it raises a contrast which is, at once, total and experimental. Human characters are always reduced in their eminence, and the impressions of awe they have raised, by a closer and more complete acquaintance. Weakness and blemish are discovered by familiarity; admiration lets in qualifiers; on approach, the halo dims a little. But it was not so with Christ. With his disciples, in closest terms of intercourse, for three whole years; their brother, friend, teacher, monitor, guest, fellow-traveler; seen by them under all the

conditions of public ministry, and private society, where the ambition of show, or the pride of power, or the ill-nature provoked by annoyance, or the vanity drawn out by confidence, would most certainly be reducing him to the criticism even of persons most unsophisticated, he is yet visibly raising their sense of his degree and quality ; becoming a greater wonder and holier mystery, and gathering to his person feelings of reverence and awe, at once more general and more sacred. Familiarity operates a kind of apotheosis, and the man becomes divinity, in simply being known.

At first, he is the Son of Mary and the Nazarene carpenter. Next, he is heard speaking with authority, as contrasted even with the Scribes. Next, he is conceived by some to be certainly Elias, or some one of the prophets, returned in power to the world. Peter takes him up, at that point, as being certainly the Christ, the great mysterious Messiah ; only not so great that he is not able to reprove him, when he begins to talk of being killed by his enemies ; protesting "be it far from thee, Lord." But the next we see of the once bold apostle, he is beckoning to another, at the table, to whisper the Lord and ask who it is that is going to betray him ; unable himself to so much as invade the sacred ear of his Master with the audible and open question. Then, shortly after, when he comes out of the hall of Caiaphas, flushed and flurried with his threefold lie, and

his base hypocrisy of cursing, what do we see but
that, simply catching the great Master's eye, his
heart breaks down, riven with insupportable anguish, and is utterly dissolved in childish tears.
And so it will be discovered in all the disciples, that
Christ is more separated from them, and holds them
in deeper awe, the closer he comes to them and the
more perfectly they know him.

The same, too, is true of his enemies. At first,
they look on him only as some new fanatic, that has
come to turn the heads of the people. Next, they
want to know whence he drew his opinions, and his
singular accomplishments in the matter of public
address ; not being, as all that knew him testify, an
educated man. Next, they send out a company to
arrest him, and, when they hear him speak, they are
so deeply impressed that they dare not do it, but
go back, under a kind of invincible awe, testifying—
"never man spake like this man." Afterward, to
break some fancied spell there may be in him, they
hire one of his own friends to betray him ; and even
then, when they come directly before him and hear
him speak, they are in such tremor of apprehension, lest he should suddenly annihilate them, that
they reel incontinently backward and are pitched
on the ground. Pilate trembles visibly before him,
and the more because of his silence and his wonderful submission. And then, when the fatal deed
is done, what do we see but that the multitude,

awed by some dread mystery in the person of the crucified, return home smiting on their breasts for anguish, in the sense of what their infatuated and guilty rage has done.

The most conspicuous matter, therefore, in the history of Jesus, is, that what holds true, in all our experience of men, is inverted in him. He grows sacred, peculiar, wonderful, Our experience of men reversed divine, as acquaintance reveals him. At in him. first he is only a man, as the senses report him to be ; knowledge, observation, familiarity, raise him into the God-man. He grows pure and perfect, more than mortal in wisdom, a being enveloped in sacred mystery, a friend to be loved in awe—dies into awe, and a sorrow that contains the element of worship! And exactly this appears in the history, without any token of art, or even apparent consciousness that it does appear—appears because it is true. Probably no one of the evangelists ever so much as noticed this remarkable inversion of what holds good respecting men, in the life and character of Jesus. Is this character human, or is it plainly divine ?

We have now sketched some of the principal distinctions of the superhuman character of Jesus. We have seen him unfolding as a flower, from the germ of a perfect youth : Recapitulation. growing up to enter into great scenes and have his part in great trials ; harmonious in all with himself and truth, a miracle of celestial beauty. He is a Lamb in innocence, a God in dignity ; revealing an impenitent but faultless piety, such as no mortal ever attempted, such as, to the highest of mortals, is inherently impossible. He advances the most extravagant pretensions, without any show of conceit, or even seeming fault of modesty. He suffers without affectation of composure and without restraint of pride ; suffers as no mortal sensibility can, and where, to mortal view, there was no reason for pain at all ; giving us not only an example of gentleness and patience in all the small trials of life, but revealing the depths even of the passive virtues of God, in his agony and the patience of his suffering love. He undertakes also a plan, universal in extent, perpetual in time ; viz., to unite all nations in a kingdom of righteousness under God ; laying his foundations in the hearts of the poor, as no great teacher had ever done before, and yet without creating ever a faction, or stirring one partisan feeling in his followers. In his teachings he is perfectly original, distinct from his age and from all ages ; never warped by the expectation of his friends ; always in a balance of truth, swayed by no excesses, running to no oppositions or extremes; clear of all superstition, and equally clear of all liberalism ; presenting the highest doctrines in the lowest and simplest forms ; establishing a pure, universal morality, never before established ; and, with all his intense devotion to the truth, never anxious, perceptibly, for the success of his doctrine. Finally, to sum up all in one, he grows more great and wise, and sacred, the more he is known—needs, in fact, to be known, to have his perfection seen. And this, we say, is Jesus, the Christ ; manifestly not human, not of our world—some being who has burst into it, and is not of it. Call him for the present, that " Holy Thing," and say, " by this we believe that thou camest from God."

Not to say that we are dissatisfied with this sketch, would be almost an irreverence of itself, to the subject of it. Who can satisfy himself with any thing that he can say of Jesus Christ ? We have seen, how many pictures of the sacred person of Jesus, by the first masters ; but not one, among them all, that did not rebuke the weakness which could dare attempt an impossible subject. So of the character of Jesus. It is necessary, for the holy interest of truth, that we should explore it, as we are best able ; but what are human thoughts and human conceptions, on a subject that dwarfs all thought and immediately outgrows whatever is conceived. And yet, for the reason that we have failed, we seem also to have succeeded. For the more impossible it is found to be, to grasp the character and set it forth, the more clearly it is seen to be above our range—a miracle and a mystery.

Two questions now remain, which our argument requires to be answered. And the first is this—did any such character, as this we have been tracing, actually exist? Admitting that the character, whether it be fact or fiction, is such as we have seen it to be, two suppositions are open ; either that such a character actually lived, and was possible to be described, because it furnished the matter of the picture, itself ; or else, that Jesus, being a merely human character as he lived, was adorned to set off in this manner, by the exaggerations of fancy, and fable, and wild tradition afterward. In the former alternative, we have the insuperable difficulty of believing, that any so perfect and glorious character was ever attained to by a mortal. If Christ was a merely natural man, then was he under all the conditions privative, as regards the security of his virtue, that we have discovered in man. He was a new-created being, as such to be perfected in a character of steadfast holiness, only by the experiment of evil and redemption from it. We can believe any miracle, therefore, more easily than that Christ was a man, and yet a perfect character, such as here is given.

In the latter alternative, we have four different writers, widely distinguished in their style and mental habit—inferior persons, all, as regards their accomplishments, and none of them remarkable for gifts of genius—contributing their parts, and coalescing thus in the representation of a character perfectly harmonious with itself, and, withal, a character whose ideal no poet had been able to create, no philosopher, by the profoundest effort of thought, to conceive and set forth to the world. What is more, these four writers are, by the supposition, children all of credulity, retailing the absurd gossip and the fabulous stories of an age of marvels, and yet, by some accident, they are found to have conceived and sketched the only perfect character known to mankind. To believe this, requires a more credulous age than these writers ever saw. We fall back, then, upon our conclusion, and there we rest. Such was the real historic character of Jesus. Thus he lived ; the character is possible to be conceived, because it was actualized in a living example. The only solution is that which is given by Jesus himself, when he says—" I came forth from the Father, and am come into the world."

The second question is this : whether this character is to be conceived as an actually existing sinless character in the world? That it is Was he a sinless character?
I maintain, because the character can no otherwise be accounted for in its known excellences. How was it that a simple-minded peasant of Galilee, was able to put himself in advance, in this manner, of all human teaching and excellence ; unfolding a character so peculiar in its combinations, and so plainly impossible to any mere man of the

race? Because his soul was filled with internal beauty and purity, having no spot, or stain, distorted by no obliquity of view or feeling, lapsing, therefore, into no eccentricity or deformity. We can make out no account of him so easy to believe, as that he was sinless; indeed, we can make no other account of him at all. He realized what are, humanly speaking, impossibilities; for his soul was warped and weakened by no human infirmities, doing all in a way of ease and naturalness, just because it is easy for clear waters to flow from a pure spring. To believe that Jesus got up these high conceptions artistically, and then acted them, in spite of the conscious disturbance of his internal harmony, and the conscious clouding of his internal purity by sin, would involve a degree of credulity and a want of perception, as regards the laws of the soul and their necessary action under sin, so lamentable as to be a proper subject of pity. We could sooner believe all the fables of the Talmud.

Besides, if Jesus was a sinner, he was conscious of sin as all sinners are, and, therefore, was a hypocrite in the whole fabric of his character; realizing so much of divine beauty in it, maintaining the show of such unfaltering harmony and celestial grace, and doing all this with a mind confused and fouled by the affectations acted for true virtues! Such an example of successful hypocrisy would be itself the greatest miracle ever heard of in the world.

Furthermore, if Jesus was a sinner, then he was, of course, a fallen being ; down under the bondage, distorted by the perversity of sin and its desolating effects, as men are. The root, therefore, of all his beauty is guilt. Evil has broken loose in him, he is held fast under evil. Bad thoughts are streaming through his soul in bad successions ; his tempers have lost their tune ; his affections have been touched by leprosy ; remorse scowls upon his heart ; his views have lost their balance and contracted obliquity ; in a word, he is fallen. Is it then such a being, one who has been touched, in this manner, by the demon spell of evil—is it he that is unfolding such a character?

What, then, do our critics in the school of naturalism say of this character of Christ? Of course they are obliged to say many handsome and almost saintly things of it. Mr. Mr. Parker's estimate of him. Parker says of him, that " He unites in himself the sublimest precepts and divinest practices, thus more than realizing the dream of prophets and sages ; rises free from all prejudice of his age, nation, or sect ; gives free range to the Spirit of God, in his breast ; sets aside the law, sacred and true—honored as it was, its forms, its sacrifice, its temple, its priests ; puts away the doctors of the law, subtle, irrefragable, and pours out a doctrine beautiful as the light, sublime as Heaven, and true as God." *

* Discourses of Religion, p. 294.

Again—as if to challenge for his doctrine, the distinction of a really supernatural excellence—" Try him as we try other teachers. They deliver their word, find a few waiting for the consolation who accept the new tidings, follow the new method, and soon go beyond their teacher, though less mighty minds than he. Though humble men, we see what Socrates and Luther never saw. But eighteen centuries have passed since the Sun of humanity rose so high in Jesus ; what man, what sect has mastered his thought, comprehended his method, and so fully applied it to life." *

Mr. Hennel, who writes in a colder mood, but has, on the whole, produced the ablest of all the argu- ments yet offered on this side, speaks more cautiously. He says, " Whilst no human character, in the history of the world, can be brought to mind, which, in proportion as it could be closely examined, did not present some defects, disqualifying it for being the emblem of moral perfection, we can rest, with least check or sense of incongruity, on the imperfectly known character of Jesus of Nazareth." †

Mr. Hennel's estimate.

But the intimation here is, that the character is not perfect ; it is only one in which the sense of perfection suffers " least check." And where is the fault charged? Why, it is discovered that Jesus cursed a fig-tree, in which he

Faults charged.

* Discourses of Religion, p. 303. † Inquiry, p. 451.

is seen to be both angry and unreasonable. He denounced the Pharisees in terms of bitter animosity. He also drove the money changers out of the temple with a scourge of rods, in which he is even betrayed into an act of physical violence. These and such like specks of fault are discovered, as they think, in the life of Jesus. So graceless in our conceit, have we of this age grown, that we can think it a point of scholarly dignity and reason, to spot the only perfect beauty that has ever graced our world, with such discovered blemishes as these! As if sin could ever need to be made out against a real sinner, in this small way of special pleading ; or as if it were ever the way of sin to err in single particles or homœopathic quantities of wrong! A more just sensibility would denounce this malignant style of criticism, as a heartless and really low-minded pleasure in letting down the honors of goodness.

In justice to Mr. Parker, it must be admitted that he does not actually charge these points of history as faults, or blemishes in the character of Jesus. And yet, in justice also, it must be added that he does compose a Faults supposed and intimated. section under the heading—"*The Negative Side, or the Limitations of Jesus,*"—where these, with other like matters, are thrown in by insinuation, as possible charges sometimes advanced by others. For himself, he alleges nothing positive, but that Jesus was under the popular delusion of his time, in respect to devils or demoniacal possessions, and that he was mistaken in some of his references to the Old Testament. What, now, is to be thought of such material, brought forward under such a heading, to flaw such a character! Is it sure that Christ was mistaken in his belief of the foul spirits? Is it certain that a sufficient mode of interpretation will not clear his references of mistake? And so, when it is suggested, at second hand, that his invective is too fierce against the Pharisees, is there no escape, but to acknowledge that, " considering his youth, it was a venial error?" Or, if there be no charge but this, " at all affecting the moral and religious character of Jesus," should not a just reverence to one whose life is so nearly faultless, constrain us to look for some more favorable construction, that takes the solitary blemish away? Is it true that invective is a necessary token of ill-nature? Are there no occasions where even holiness will be most forward in it? And when a single man stands out alone, facing a whole living order and caste, that rule the time—oppressors of the poor, hypocrites and pretenders in religion, corrupters of all truth and faith, under the names of learning and religion—is the malediction, the woe, that he hurls against them, to be taken as a fault of violence and unregulated passion ; or considering what amount of force and public influence he dares to confront and set in deadly enmity against his person, is he rather to be accepted as God's champion, in the honors of a great and genuinely heroic spirit?

Considering how fond the world is of invective, how ready to admire the rhetoric of sharp words, how many speakers study to excel in the fine art of excoriation, how many reformers are applauded in vehement His invective against the Pharisees. attacks on character, and win a great repute of fearlessness, just because of their severity, when, in fact, there is nothing to fear—when possibly the subject is a dead man, not yet buried—it is really a most striking tribute to the more than human character of Jesus, that we are found to be so apprehensive respecting him in particular, lest his plain, unstudied, unrhetorical severities on this or that occasion, may imply some possible defect, or "venial error," in him. Why this special sensibility to fault in him? save that, by his beautiful and perfect life, he has raised our conceptions so high as to make, what we might applaud in a man, a possible blemish in his divine excellence?

The glorious old reformer and blind poet of Puritanism—vindicator of a free commonwealth and a free, unprelatical religion—holds, in our view, a far worthier and manlier conception of Christ's dealing with the Pharisees, and Milton's right of invective. of what is due to all the usurpations of titled conceit and oppression in the world. With truly refreshing vehemence, he writes—"For in times of opposition, when against new heresies arising, or old corruptions to be reformed, this cool, impassionate mildness of positive wisdom, is not enough to damp and astonish the proud resistance of carnal and false doctors, then (that I may have leave to soar awhile, as the poets use,) Zeal, whose substance is ethereal, arming in complete diamond, ascends his fiery chariot, drawn by two blazing meteors figured like beasts, but of a higher breed than any the zodiac yields, resembling those four which Ezekiel and St. John saw—the one visaged like a lion, to express power, high authority, and indignation ; the other of man, to cast derision and scorn upon perverse and fraudulent seducers—with them the invincible warrior, Zeal, shaking loosely the slack reins, drives over the heads of scarlet prelates and such as are insolent to maintain traditions, bruising their stiff necks under his flaming wheels.   Thus did the true prophets of old combat with the false ; thus Christ, himself the fountain of meekness, found acrimony enough to be still galling and vexing the prelatical Pharisees.   But ye will say, these had immediate warrant from God to be thus bitter ; and I say, so much the plainer is it found that there may be a sanctified bitterness against the enemies of the truth." *

Probably Christ himself had no other account to give of his conduct, on the occasion referred to ;

* Apology for Smectymnus, Sect. I.

and no other was needed, than that he felt a zeal
within him (answering to Milton's picture), which
could not, must not be repressed. His disciples felt
his terrible severity, and were going to be shocked
by it, but they remembered the Scripture—"The
zeal of thy house hath eaten me up." After all, it
was, when rightly viewed, the necessary outburst,
only, of that indignant fire, which is kindled in the
sweet bosom of innocence, by the insolence of hypocrisy and oppression.

I conclude, then, (1.) that Christ actually lived,
and bore the real character ascribed to him in the
history. And (2.) that he was a sinless character.
How far off is he now from any possible classifica-
tion in the genus humanity!

Here, then, is a being who has broken into the
world, and is not of it ; one who has come out from
God, and is even an expression to us of The fact of his
the complete beauty of God—such as miracles implied.
he should be, if he actually was, what he is affirmed
to be, the Eternal Word of the Father incarnate.
Did he work miracles? This now is the question
that waits for our decision—did he work miracles?
By the supposition, he is superhuman. By the
supposition, too, he is in the world as a miracle.
Agreeing that the laws of nature will not be sus-
pended, any more than they are by our own supernatural action, will they yet be so subordinated to

his power, as to permit the performance of signs and wonders, in which we may recognize a super-human force? Since he is shown to be a superhuman being, manifestly nature will have a relation to him, under and by her own laws, such as accords with his superhuman quality, and it will be very singular if he does not do superhuman things; nay, it is even philosophically incredible that he should not, and that without any breach upon the integrity of nature. Thus an organ is a certain instrument, curiously framed or adjusted in its parts, and prepared to yield itself to any force which touches the keys. An animal runs back and forth across the key-board, and produces a jarring, disagreeable jumble of sounds. Thereupon he begins to reason, and convinces himself that it is in the nature of the instrument to make such sounds, and no other. But a skilful player comes to the instrument, as a higher presence, endowed with a super-animal sense and skill. He strikes the keys, and all-melodious and heavenly sounds roll out upon the enchanted air. Will the animal now go on to reason that this is impossible, incredible, because it violates the nature of the instrument, and is contrary to his own experience? Perhaps he may, and men may sometimes not be wiser than he. But the player himself, and all that can think it possible for him to do what the animal can not, will have no doubt that the music is made by the same laws that made the jargon. Just so Christ, to whose will or touch the mundane system is pliant as to ours, may be able to execute results through its very laws subordinated to him, which to us are impossible. Nay, it would be itself a contradiction of all order and fit relation if he could not. To suppose that a being out of humanity, will be shut up within all the limitations of humanity, is incredible, and contrary to reason. The very laws of nature themselves, having him present to them, as a new agent and higher first term, would require the development of new consequences and incidents, in the nature of wonders. Being a miracle himself, it would be the greatest of all miracles if he did not work miracles.

Let it be further noted, that Christ is here on an errand high enough to justify his appearing, and also of a nature to exclude any suspicion His errand is that he is going to overthrow the order order itself. of God's works. He declares that he has come out from God, to be a restorer of sin, a regenerator of all things, a new moral creator of the world ; thus to do a work that is, at once, the hope of all order, and the greatest of all miracles. He tells us, indeed, that he is come to set up the kingdom of God, and fulfil the highest ends of the divine goodness in the creation of the world itself ; and the dignity of his work, certified by the dignity also of his character, sets all things in proportion, and commends him to our confidence in all the wonders he performs.

Nor shall we apprehend in his miracles any disruption of law ; for we shall see that he is executing
that true system, above nature and
more comprehensive, which is itself the
basis of all stability, and contains the real import of
all things. Dwelling from eternity in this higher
system himself, and having it centred in his person,
wheeling and subordinating thus all physical instru-
ments, as doubtless he may, to serve those better
ends in which all order lies, it will not be in us,
when he comes forth from the Father, on the
Father's errand, to forbid that he shall work in the
prerogatives of the Father. Visibly not one of us,
but a visitant who has come out from a realm of
spiritual majesty, back of the sensuous orb on which
our moth-eyes dwell as in congenial dimness and
obscurity of light, what shall we think when we see
diseases fly before him, and blindness letting fall
the scales of obscured vision, and death retreating
from its prey, but that the seeming disruption of
our retributive state under sin, is made to let in
mercy and order from above ? For, if man has
buried himself in sense, and married all sense to
sin, which sin is itself the soul of all disorder, can
it be to us a frightful thing that he lays his hand
upon the perverted casualties, and says, "thou art
made whole ?" If the bad empire, the bitter un-
nature of our sin, is somewhere touched by his
healing power, must we apprehend some fatal shock

No disruption
of law or system.

of disorder? If, by his miraculous force, some crevice is made in the senses, to let in the light of heaven's peace and order, must we tremble lest the scientific laws are shaken, and the scientific causes violated? Better is it to say—"This beginning of miracles did Jesus make in Galilee, and manifested forth his glory, and we believe in him." Glory breaks in through his incarnate person, to chase away the darkness. In him, peace and order descend to rebuild the realm below, they have maintained above. Sin, the damned miracle and misery of the groaning creation, yields to the stronger miracle of Jesus and his works, and the great good minds of this and the upper worlds behold integrity and rest returning, and the peace of universal empire secure. Out of the disorder that was, rises order ; out of chaos, beauty. Amen! Alleluia! for the Lord God omnipotent reigneth!

At the same time, it must not be overlooked, that the account which is made of the Christian miracles, by the critics who deny them, is itself impossible. It is that they are myths, or legendary tales, that grew up out of the story-telling and marvelling habit of the disciples of Christ, within the first thirty years after their Master's death. They were developed, in other words, in the lifetime of the eye-witnesses of Christ's ministry, and recorded by eye-witnesses themselves. We are also required to believe that

The mythical hypothesis impossible.

four common men are able to preserve such a character as that of Christ, while loading down the history thus, with so many mythical wonders that are the garb of their very grotesque and childish credulity! By what accident, then, we are compelled to ask, was an age of myths and fables able to develop and set forth the only conception of a perfect character ever known in our world? Were these four mythological dreamers, believing their own dreams and all others beside, the men to produce the perfect character of Jesus, and a system of teachings that transcend all other teachings ever given to the race? If there be a greater miracle, or a tax on human credulity more severe, we know not where it is. Nothing is so difficult, all human literature testifies, as to draw a character, and keep it in its living proportions. How much more to draw a perfect character, and not discolor it fatally by marks from the imperfection of the biographer. How is it, then, that four humble men, in an age of marvels and Rabbinical exaggerations, have done it—done what none, not even the wisest and greatest of mankind, have ever been able to do?

So far, even Mr. Parker concedes the right of my argument. "Measure," he says, "the religious doctrine of Jesus by that of the time and place he lived in, or that of any time and any place. Yes, by the doctrine of eternal truth. Consider what a work his words and

Their success Mr. Parker concedes.

deeds have wrought in the world. Remember that the greatest minds have seen no farther, and added nothing to the doctrine of religion ; that the richest hearts have felt no deeper, and added nothing to the sentiment of religion ; have set no loftier aim, no truer method than his, of perfect love to God and man. Measure him by the shadow he has cast into the world—no, by the light he has shed upon it. Shall we be told such a man never lived ? the whole story is a lie ? Suppose that Plato and Newton never lived. But who did their wonders, and who thought their thought ? It takes a Newton to forge a Newton. What man could have fabricated a Jesus? None but a Jesus." *

Exactly so. And yet, in the middle of the very paragraph from which these words are gleaned, Mr. Parker says, " We can learn few facts about Jesus"; also, that in certain things—to wit, his miracles, we suppose—" Hercules was his equal, and Vishnu his superior." Few facts about Jesus ! all the miracles recited of him, as destitute of credibility as the stories of Hercules and Vishnu ! And yet these evangelists, retailing so many absurd fictions and so much childish gossip, have been able to give us a doctrine upon which the world has never advanced, a character so deep that the richest hearts have felt nothing deeper, and added nothing to the sentiment of it. They have done, that is, the difficult thing, and

* Life of Jesus, p. 363.

broken down under the easy! preserved, in the life and discourses of Jesus, what exceeds all human philosophy, all mortal beauty, and yet have not been able to recite the simplest facts! Is it so that any intelligent critic will reason?

Neither let it be objected that, since the miracles have in themselves no moral quality, there is no ra-

The miracles are in place in a gospel.

tional, or valuable, or even proper place for them in a gospel, considered as a new-creating grace for the world. For it is a thing of no secondary importance for a sinner, down under sin, and held fast in its bitter terms of bondage, to see that God has entered into his case with a force that is adequate. These mighty works of Jesus, which have been done and duly certified, are fit expressions to us of the fact that he can do for us all that we want. Doubtless it is a great and difficult thing to regenerate a fallen nature ; no person, really awake to his miserable and dreadful bondage, ever thought otherwise. But he that touched the blind eyes and commanded the leprosy away, he that trod the sea, and raised the dead, and burst the bars of death himself, can tame the passions, sweeten the bitter affections, regenerate the inbred diseases, and roll back all the storms of the mind. Assured in this manner by his miracles, they become arguments of trust, a storehouse of powerful images, that invigorate courage and stimulate hope. Broken as we are by our sorrow, cast down as we are by our guiltiness, ashamed, and weak, and ready to despair, we can yet venture a hope that our great soul-miracle may be done ; that, if we can but touch the hem of Christ's garment, a virtue will go out of him to heal us. In all dark days and darker struggles of the mind, in all outward disasters, and amid all storms upon the sea of life, we can yet descry him treading the billows, and hear him saying, "It is I, be not afraid." And lest we should believe the miracles faintly, for there is a busy infidel lurking always in our hearts to cheat us of our faith, when he cannot reason it away, the character of Jesus is ever shining with and through them, in clear self-evidence, leaving them never to stand as raw wonders only of might, but covering them with glory, as tokens of a heavenly love, and acts that only suit the proportions of his personal greatness and majesty.

There are many in our day, as we know, who, without making any speculative point of the objection we are discussing, have so far Miracles rejected, so is Jesus the Grand Miracle. yielded to the current misbelief as to profess, with a certain air of self-compliment, that they are quite content to accept the spirit of Jesus ; and let the miracles go for what they are worth. Little figure will they make as Christians in that kind of gospel. They will not, in fact, receive the spirit of Jesus ; for that, unabridged, is itself the Grand Miracle of Christianity,

about which all the others play as scintillations only
of the central fire. Still less will they believe that
Jesus can do any thing in them which their sin requires. They will only compliment his beauty, imi-
tate or ape his ways in a feeble lifting of themselves,
but that he can roll back the currents of nature,
loosened by the disorders of sin, and raise them to
a new birth in holiness, they will not believe. No
such watery gospel of imitation, separated from
grace, will have any living power in their life, or
set them in any bond of unity with God. Nothing
but to say—"Jesus of Nazareth, a man approved of
God by miracles and signs which God did by him,"
can draw the soul to faith, and open it to the power
of a supernatural and new-creative mercy.

We come back, then, to the self-evidencing superhuman character of Jesus, and there we rest.

Jesus himself
the all-sufficient
evidence.

He is the sun that holds all the minor
orbs of revelation to their places, and
pours a sovereign, self-evidencing light
into all religious knowledge. We have been debating much, and ranging over a wide field, in chase
of the many phantoms of doubt and false argument,
still we have not far to go for light, if only we could
cease debating and sit down to see. It is no in-
genious fetches of argument that we want ; no external testimony, gathered here and there from the
records of past ages, suffices to end our doubts ;
but it is the new sense opened in us by Jesus him-

self—a sense deeper than words and more immediate than inference—of the miraculous grandeur of his life ; a glorious agreement felt between his works and his person, such that his miracles themselves are proved to us in our feeling, believed in by that inward testimony. On this inward testimony we are willing to stake every thing, even the life that now is, and that which is to come. If the miracles, if revelation itself, can not stand upon the superhuman character of Jesus, then let it fall. If that character does not contain all truth and centralize all truth in itself, then let there be no truth. If there is any thing worthy of belief not found in this, we may well consent to live and die without it. Before this sovereign light, streaming out from God, the deep questions, and dark surmises, and doubts unresolved, which make a night so gloomy and terrible about us, hurry away to their native abyss. God, who commanded the light to shine out of darkness, hath shined in our hearts, to give the light of the knowledge of the glory of God in the face of Jesus Christ. This it is that has conquered the assaults of doubt and false learning in all past ages, and will in all ages to come. No argument against the sun will drive it from the sky. No mole-eyed skepticism, dazzled by its brightness, can turn away the shining it refuses to look upon. And they who long after God, will be ever turning their eyes thitherward, and either with reason or without reason, or, if need be, against manifold impediments of reason, will see and believe.

———

But before we drop a theme like this, let us note more distinctly the immense significance to our religious feeling of this glorious advent of Jesus, and have our congratulations in it. This one perfect character has come into our world, and lived in it; filling all the molds of action, all the terms of duty and love, with his own divine manners, works and charities. All the conditions of our life are raised thus, by the meaning he has shown to be in them, and the grace he has put upon them. The world itself is changed, and is no more the same that it was; it has never been the same since Jesus left it. The air is charged with heavenly odors, and a kind of celestial consciousness, a sense of other worlds, is wafted on us in its breath. Let the dark ages come, let society roll backward and churches perish in whole regions of the earth, let infidelity deny, and, what is worse, let spurious piety dishonor the truth; still there is a something here that was not, and a something that has immortality in it. Still our confidence remains unshaken, that Christ and his all-quickening life are in the world, as fixed elements, and will be to the end of time; for Christianity is not so much the advent of a better doctrine, as of a perfect character; and how can a perfect character, once entered into life and history, be separated and finally expelled? It were easier to untwist all the beams of light in the sky, separating and expunging one of the colors, than to get the character of Jesus, which is the real gospel, out of the world. Look ye hither, meantime, all ye blinded and fallen of mankind, a better nature is among you, a pure heart, out of some pure world, is come into your prison and walks it with you. Do you require of us to show who he is, and definitely to expound his person? We may not be able. Enough to know that he is not of us—some strange being out of nature and above it, whose name is Wonderful. Enough that sin has never touched his hallowed nature, and that he is a friend. In him dawns a hope—purity has not come into the world, except to purify. Behold the Lamb of God, that taketh away the sins of the world! Light breaks in, peace settles on the air, lo! the prison walls are giving way—rise, let us go.

THE END.

PRESS OF
EDWARD O. JENKINS' SONS,
NEW YORK